A 31 Day Love Transformation Prayer Devotional

Healing A Broken Spirit From The Inside Out

TAYNIA A. MOSLEY

FOREWORD

Taynia Mosley is a beautiful woman of God, wife, mother, author and relationship specialist. She has so many gifts and talents on the inside of her. She loves to use those very same gifts and talents for the Glory of Christ.

When it comes to empowering others, Taynia leads by example. She is dedicated to helping others to build their relationship with God.

It is a delight to commend **Taynia** on *A 31 Day Love Transformational* on her newest book. The book is filled with prayers, daily scriptures, affirmations and more. As you read this book it is going to inspire you to influence in more daily prayer and reflections. I am excited to see her progress and growth thus far.

As I began my own personal relationship with God over twenty years ago, I read many books on prayer. However, I found that workbooks on prayer helped me the best in progressing in my walk with God. I am a living testimony that applying prayer, scriptures, and affirmations daily will begin to change the way we all think and act. I encourage my family, friends congregation, anyone, to incorporate these principles into their daily devotion.

Shauntae Warren

~Prophetess Shauntae Warren

This prayer devotional was created to be used as a daily sacred time with God that includes prayer, affirmations, bible scriptures, and journaling. Take one day at a time and focus on that, after you have said your daily affirmations and your daily scriptures, please take time afterward to write a letter to yourself and write what you hear from God or write a prayer to God pouring out your heart on the subject. This process will help bring clarity and understanding while clearing out your thoughts and clutter. It will give you more directions concerning your life in this season. You may use this book monthly until you get a personal breakthrough. After the first use of it, you can pray your own prayers or letters that you have written and incorporate that into your daily work.

Definitions (tools) according to the Oxford and the Merriam Webster Dictionary:

Affirmation – 1. the action or process of affirming something or being informed. 2. Emotional support or encouragement.

Journaling – a daily record of news and events of a personal nature; a diary.

Prayer – a solemn request for help or expression of thanks addressed to God or an object of worship.

Scripture – a body of writings considered sacred or authoritative.

Copyright © 2020 by Taynia A. Mosley
Publisher: Destined With A Purpose
Location: Roseville, MI
All rights reserved.
ISBN: 978-0-578-64139-3
E-book ASIN: B084D5SCNK
Library of Congress Control Number:
2020902005

Some of the affirmations were created by the author, and some were used from www.thelawofattraction.com. The Bible verses are from the Holy Bible AMP, KJV, NIV, and NLT versions of the YouVersion Holy Bible application version 2,035.

DEDICATION

This book is dedicated to those who have been brokenhearted, abused, and/or those who have lost all hope and given up on love. This road is not an easy one, it is tough, but it is not ok to feel numb. It is not ok to feel stuck with no way out. It is not ok to give up on yourself because you have been brainwashed to believe that you deserved a heartbreak.

YOU HAVE TO CHOOSE YOU, TODAY!!

No more pity parties for yourself. Grab your bootstraps and get ready to pull yourself out of the darkness that you call light. That is not what God intended for you. Yes, you went through some gut-wrenching situations, but it was all a lesson. Look at everything in your life as a lesson, you went through it so that you can be stronger, and teach others what not to do. Yes, you went through it, but it was not for you; it was meant for you to pull the next person out. Get ready for this 31-day heart transformation. It is time to DO THE WORK!!

-Coach Taynia

ACKNOWLEDGMENTS

To my wonderful husband, Rasheem Mosley, who has taught me how to love myself, honor myself, and respect myself when I lost all hope. You have no idea, but God. I thank God for you showing up when you did. I love you!

Christian, April, and Lauren, thank you for helping me find myself in my darkest moments in life. I love you girls.

To my parents Roderick and Mablene Gillison and siblings, thanks for always being there. You are always on time, even when you have no clue what is going on.

Apostle Wes and Pastor Shauntae Warren, to my church family you came to me in a season where I was soul searching and looking for more in life I am so glad we have connected. I thank you for all of your prayers.

Most of all, I give thanks to the Lord, for giving me this idea and downloading in me what I needed to give to you all. I love you, Father.

TABLE OF CONTENTS

DAY 1 I LOVE MYSELF.. 1

DAY 2 "I FORGIVE MYSELF & I FORGIVE OTHERS."................. 7

DAY 3 "I OPEN MY HEART TO RECEIVE LOVE BECAUSE I KNOW THAT I DESERVE IT".. 14

DAY 4 "I HAVE THE POWER TO GIVE LOVE ENDLESSLY." 21

DAY 5 "I AM THANKFUL FOR THE LOVE IN MY LIFE, AND I AM THANKFUL FOR MY CARING PARTNER."............................... 27

DAY 6 "I AM LOVE." 34

DAY 7 "I ATTRACT LOVING AND CARING PEOPLE INTO MY LIFE.".. 40

DAY 8 "MY LOVE GROWS STRONGER EVERY DAY."............. 46

DAY 9 "I GIVE LOVE SO I SHALL RECEIVE LOVE." 53

DAY 10 "WHEREVER I GO AND WHOMEVER I AM WITH I FIND LOVE.".. 60

DAY 11 "I ONLY THINK POSITIVE THOUGHTS ABOUT LOVE."66

DAY 12 "I SPREAD LOVE TO THOSE ALL-AROUND ME."........ 72

DAY 13 "I RADIATE UNCONDITIONAL LOVE.".......................79

DAY 14 "I AM NEEDED. I HAVE WORK TO DO!" 85

DAY 15 "I AM VALUABLE!"... 91

DAY 16 "I AM FILLED WITH THE VIBRATION OF LOVE!" 97

DAY 17 "I WELCOME LOVE WITH OPEN ARMS"................. 104

DAY 18 "I DESERVE LOVE AND RECEIVE IT IN ABUNDANCE" 110

DAY 19 "LOVE IS ATTRACTED TO ME, AND I AM ATTRACTED

TO LOVE" 117

DAY 20 "LOVE FOLLOWS ME EVERYWHERE THAT I GO" 124

DAY 21 "LOVE IS THE MOTIVE" 131

DAY 22 "I DWELL IN LOVE." 138

DAY 23 "I AM CREATED FOR LOVE" 144

DAY 24 "I FEEL LOVED" 151

DAY 25 "I KNOW THAT I AM ENOUGH. I SHOW UP FOR MYSELF AND OTHERS" 158

DAY 26 "I ONLY ATTRACT HEALTHY, LOVING RELATIONSHIPS" 165

DAY 27 "I AM SELFLESS" 172

DAY 28 "I AM WORTHY OF LOVE" 179

DAY 29 "I AM HEALED" 186

DAY 30 "I AM WHOLE. I AM COMPLETE." 193

DAY 31 I AM DIVINE LOVE 200

A 31 Day Love Transformation Prayer Devotional

DAY 1

I LOVE MYSELF

Look in the mirror and stand tall, hold your head up high and tell yourself, "I love you" and truly mean it. Repeat it until you can feel it deep down in your soul; in your spirit.

> *Whoever pursues righteousness and love finds life, prosperity, and honor.*
>
> *Proverbs 21:21 NIV*

Lord God, help me to find it in myself to love myself as you love the church. I forgive myself for any wrongdoings and or harm that I have caused to myself. Lord, help me to know that I am loved and that most of all, you love me. Help me to forgive myself so that I can forgive others, and others may forgive me.

I love you _____, I love you_____, I love you_____. May I never forget that I am loved, I am needed, and I am valuable. Help me to continue to speak life over myself in every situation. In Jesus' Name. Amen.

Taynia a. Mosley

"I LOVE MYSELF."

A 31 Day Love Transformation Prayer Devotional

Love Letter to Self

Taynia a. Mosley

A 31 Day Love Transformation Prayer Devotional

Love letter to God

Taynia a. Mosley

A 31 Day Love Transformation Prayer Devotional

DAY 2
"I FORGIVE MYSELF & I FORGIVE OTHERS."

I forgive myself. I forgive myself. I forgive myself. I forgive those who have offended, wronged, or hurt me.

Ready, Set, Go!

Since God chose you to be the holy people he loves, you must clothe yourselves with tenderhearted mercy, kindness, humility, gentleness, and patience. Make allowance for each other's faults, and forgive anyone who offends you. Remember, the Lord forgave you, so you must forgive others. Above all, clothe yourself with love, which binds us all together in perfect harmony. And let the peace that comes from Christ rule in your hearts. For as members of one body, you are called to live in peace. And always be thankful.

Colossians 3:12-15 NLT

Dear Heavenly Father, I have not done everything right in my life, and sometimes I hold myself hostage for it. Lord, I need your help with forgiveness for myself and for others that have hurt me or wronged me in the past. Help me to forgive in my heart, and I mean REALLY forgive by letting the matter go. I do not wish to hold this burden of hurt, pain, anger, fear and/or unforgiveness in my heart. For your word tells me to forgive in order to be forgiven, so I choose to forgive. I pray to be cleansed from the unforgiveness of past situations. I pray to be able to forgive myself in every situation. I pray to be able to forgive others with no hard feelings, with no hesitation. I don't want to be upset with anyone or hold harsh feelings towards anyone. Help me to let it all go. I pray that love conquers all because love is what makes us. I thank you, Father, and it is so. In Jesus' Mighty Name, I Pray. Amen.

A 31 Day Love Transformation Prayer Devotional

"I FORGIVE MYSELF & I FORGIVE OTHERS."

Taynia a. Mosley

Love Letter to Self

_____
_____
_____
_____
_____
_____
_____
_____
_____
_____
_____
_____
_____
_____
_____
_____
_____
_____
_____
_____
_____
_____
_____
_____
_____

A 31 Day Love Transformation Prayer Devotional

Love letter to God

A 31 Day Love Transformation Prayer Devotional

DAY 3

"I OPEN MY HEART TO RECEIVE LOVE BECAUSE I KNOW THAT I DESERVE IT"

Today take a deep look at yourself in the mirror and focus on receiving love on today. Repeat and Affirm to yourself:

Such love has no fear because perfect love expels all fear. If we are afraid, it is for fear of punishment, and this shows that we have not fully experienced his perfect love. We love each other because he loved us first.

1 John:18-19 NLT

Jesus, I come to you as humble as I can, asking that you forgive me for only seeing the good in myself and never taking the time to acknowledge other people in their good doings. Help me to see past the hurt, pain, and confusion so that I can understand that I deserve to receive love. Lord, I open my heart on this day to receive the love that I deserve, I receive the love that I have blocked out of my life because I did not want to be hurt again. I thank you for a new heart today. I thank you, Father, that it is done. In Jesus' Name, we pray. Amen.

Taynia a. Mosley

"I OPEN MY HEART TO RECEIVE LOVE BECAUSE I KNOW THAT I DESERVE LOVE."

A 31 Day Love Transformation Prayer Devotional

Love Letter to Self

Taynia a. Mosley

A 31 Day Love Transformation Prayer Devotional

Love letter to God

Taynia a. Mosley

DAY 4
"I HAVE THE POWER TO GIVE LOVE ENDLESSLY."

Today I want you to get in front of the mirror and repeat the affirmation until you believe the words that are coming off of your lips.

For the Spirit God gave us does not make us timid, but gives us power, love, and self-discipline.

2 Timothy 1:7 NIV

Today I pray for the spirit of love to fall upon me like never before. I want to love my enemies, I want to love my family, friends, neighbors, and people that I connect with daily. Lord, help me to be your shining light through the power of love and forgiveness. Oh God, cleanse my heart, for I have the power to love endlessly without fear. In Jesus' Name. Amen.

> "I HAVE THE POWER TO GIVE LOVE ENDLESSLY."

A 31 Day Love Transformation Prayer Devotional

Love Letter to Self

Taynia a. Mosley

A 31 Day Love Transformation Prayer Devotional

Love letter to God

_____
_____
_____
_____
_____
_____
_____
_____
_____
_____
_____
_____
_____
_____
_____
_____
_____
_____
_____
_____
_____
_____
_____
_____

Taynia a. Mosley

DAY 5

"I AM THANKFUL FOR THE LOVE IN MY LIFE, AND I AM THANKFUL FOR MY CARING PARTNER."

We are doing the work today. The bible says to speak those things that are not as though they were. If this affirmation is a challenge for you, then I challenge you to dig deep and focus on what you want and deserve. Say it aloud in the mirror until you feel it.

When I said, "My foot is slipping," your unfailing love, Lord, supported me.

Psalm 94:18 NIV

God, I thank you for your unfailing love that supports me even when I don't know how to support myself. I thank you for loving me even when I don't know how to love myself or others. I thank you, Lord God, for the love that is already flourishing in my life and the love of my spouse. I am so thankful for my loving, caring, affectionate spouse. God, you have given me everything I have ever needed. I just want to say thank you, and I love you, Lord. Amen.

A 31 Day Love Transformation Prayer Devotional

"I AM THANKFUL FOR THE LOVE IN MY LIFE, AND I AM THANKFUL FOR MY CARING PARTNER."

Taynia a. Mosley

Love Letter to Self

_____
_____
_____
_____
_____
_____
_____
_____
_____
_____
_____
_____
_____
_____
_____
_____
_____
_____
_____
_____
_____
_____
_____
_____

A 31 Day Love Transformation Prayer Devotional

Love letter to God

A 31 Day Love Transformation Prayer Devotional

DAY 6
"I AM LOVE."

Today grab that mirror and repeat this affirmation and mean it. Everywhere that you go, love should drip off of your countenance like never before.

Keep on loving one another as brothers and sisters. Do not forget to show hospitality to strangers, for by so doing, some people have shown hospitality to angels without knowing it.

Hebrews 13:1-2 NIV

Whomever I come in to contact with today, Lord, let them feel your presence, let them feel your anointing and, most importantly, let them feel your love. I want people to witness this feeling of love that you have enwrapped upon my life. Lord God bring peace in this season as your love overflow into our hearts. In Jesus' Name. Amen.

A 31 Day Love Transformation Prayer Devotional

"I AM LOVE."

Love Letter to Self

A 31 Day Love Transformation Prayer Devotional

Taynia a. Mosley

Love letter to God

A 31 Day Love Transformation Prayer Devotional

DAY 7

"I ATTRACT LOVING AND CARING PEOPLE INTO MY LIFE."

Jump in front of the mirror and repeat. Repeat. Repeat.

For this very reason, make every effort to add to your faith goodness; and to goodness, knowledge; and to knowledge, self-control; and to self-control, perseverance; and to perseverance, godliness; and to godliness, mutual affection; and to mutual affection love.

2 Peter 1:5-7 NIV

I pray for the loving and caring people that are in my life and those that will come into my life. I pray for their strength to love, even when they don't know how to. I pray a hedge of protection around them, Father, that they will not lose sight but keep their eyes on you. I pray that you order their footsteps in this season and that your light of love shine brightly upon them. In Jesus' Name. Amen.

A 31 Day Love Transformation Prayer Devotional

"I ATTRACT LOVING AND CARING PEOPLE INTO MY LIFE."

Taynia a. Mosley

Love Letter to Self

A 31 Day Love Transformation Prayer Devotional

Love letter to God

A 31 Day Love Transformation Prayer Devotional

DAY 8

"MY LOVE GROWS STRONGER EVERY DAY."

Mirror work: get in the mirror and repeat this affirmation for 5 minutes today. You have to feel that your love is growing stronger each and every day. Your love is growing for yourself and others because many people will need to feel your love today.

Whoever has my commands and keeps them is the one who loves me. The one who loves me will be loved by my Father, and I too will love them and show myself to them.

John 14:21 NIV

In my weakest hour, Lord, I ask that you step in and comfort me, oh, God. Comfort my spirit and my soul with the spirit of love. In my darkest hours, I ask that you pour out your love upon me, help me to grow in you. Help me to see your love for me every single day and help me to be love to those that don't feel loved or needed. Help me to comfort others in their low and dark moments. Lord, I give you all the praise and all the glory for what you are doing in my life. In Jesus' Name. Amen.

"MY LOVE GROWS STRONGER EVERY DAY."

A 31 Day Love Transformation Prayer Devotional

Love Letter to Self

Taynia a. Mosley

A 31 Day Love Transformation Prayer Devotional

Love letter to God

Taynia a. Mosley

DAY 9

"I GIVE LOVE SO I SHALL RECEIVE LOVE."

Let's head to the mirror and say this affirmation over and over again, repeat it throughout your day, and even before you go to sleep. As you move through the day, this affirmation will be a reminder to you and bring you peace in every situation. Love conquers all…God is Love, and so are you!

Most important of all, continue to show deep love for each other, for love covers a multitude of sins.

1 Peter 4:8 NLT

Lord, hear my cry unto you today. I cry out to be love to everyone and every situation that I come into contact with. I know that I am not perfect, but you see past that and you still love me; you still give me a chance to get it right. Father, I ask for your grace to fall upon me so that I can give grace to those that I come in contact with today. Help me to be forgiving as you are forgiving of your people. I do realize that I am in no position to hold grudges, resentment, or judgment, for I am not perfect, so I should not expect that from others. Help me to be humbled in this season, help me to show love to those who need it. Help me to show love to someone who needs love today. In Jesus' Name, I pray. Amen.

A 31 Day Love Transformation Prayer Devotional

"I GIVE LOVE SO I SHALL RECEIVE LOVE."

Taynia a. Mosley

Love Letter to Self

_____
_____
_____
_____
_____
_____
_____
_____
_____
_____
_____
_____
_____
_____
_____
_____
_____
_____
_____
_____
_____

A 31 Day Love Transformation Prayer Devotional

Taynia a. Mosley

Love letter to God

A 31 Day Love Transformation Prayer Devotional

DAY 10

"WHEREVER I GO AND WHOMEVER I AM WITH I FIND LOVE."

Let's go to the mirror and look ourselves in the eyes and repeat. Repeat. Repeat. Today stand in your truth, accept it, acknowledge and own it, wherever you go, you find love.

I have made you known to them and will continue to make you known in order that the love you have for me may be in them and that I, myself, may be in them.

John 17:26 NIV

Sometimes I find it hard to show love around people, places, or things because I struggle with being the best version of myself. Sometimes I have a hard time forgiving myself, but I thank you, Father, for your love because it reminds me that I am forgiven. It helps me stand firm in order to show love wherever I may go. It is imperative that I show love every step of the way. I want to help others feel your love and your peace inside of their lives. Thank you for trusting me. In Jesus' Name, I pray.   Amen.

A 31 Day Love Transformation Prayer Devotional

"WHEREVER I GO AND WHOMEVER I AM WITH, I FIND LOVE."

Taynia a. Mosley

Love Letter to Self

A 31 Day Love Transformation Prayer Devotional

Taynia a. Mosley

Love letter to God

A 31 Day Love Transformation Prayer Devotional

DAY 11

"I ONLY THINK POSITIVE THOUGHTS ABOUT LOVE."

Mirror Work, Let's Do It!

Love is patient, love is kind. It does not envy, it does not boast, it is not proud. It does not dishonor others, it is not self-seeking, it is not easily angered, it keeps no record of wrongs. Love does not delight in evil but rejoices with the truth. It always protects, always trusts, always hopes, always perseveres.

1 Corinthians 13:4-7 NIV

Father, your love is patient and your love is kind; your love means everything to me. Your love conquers all, and I just want to be in your presence. I don't want to do anything without you. I want to learn how not to be boastful or proud because I want to show genuine love. Lord, your love helps guide me in my darkest moments because it helps me to see myself for who I really am in you. Thank you for helping me, thank you for keeping me. I adore you, Lord. Thank you, Father. I AM LOVE. In Jesus' Name, I Pray. Amen.

A 31 Day Love Transformation Prayer Devotional

"I ONLY THINK POSITIVE THOUGHTS ABOUT LOVE."

Taynia a. Mosley

Love Letter to Self

_____
_____
_____
_____
_____
_____
_____
_____
_____
_____
_____
_____
_____
_____
_____
_____
_____
_____
_____
_____
_____
_____

A 31 Day Love Transformation Prayer Devotional

Love letter to God

A 31 Day Love Transformation Prayer Devotional

DAY 12

"I SPREAD LOVE TO THOSE ALL-AROUND ME."

Hop in front of the mirror, and let's get to it! Repeat the daily affirmation to yourself and look deep into your soul while saying it. Say it until you feel good about it. Say it until you truly mean what you are proclaiming that you spread love to those all around you because you are love.

Create in me a pure heart, O God, and renew a steadfast spirit within me. Do not cast me from your presence or take your Holy Spirit from me. Restore to me the joy of your salvation and grant me a willing spirit, to sustain me.

Psalms 51:10-12 NIV

Jesus, I ask that you touch my heart today and show me where I need to go and whom I need to talk to. People are searching for you but do not know how to listen for your voice because they feel that you are so far away. Help me to show your light to those people that feel lost today. I want to show them your love,

Father, because somehow, they have lost their way. Guide me with the right words to say just what they need to hear today. Lord, I thank you for loving us, your people. In Jesus' Name, I Pray. Amen.

Taynia a. Mosley

"I SPREAD LOVE TO THOSE ALL-AROUND ME."

A 31 Day Love Transformation Prayer Devotional

Love Letter to Self

Taynia a. Mosley

A 31 Day Love Transformation Prayer Devotional

Love letter to God

Taynia a. Mosley

DAY 13

"I RADIATE UNCONDITIONAL LOVE."

I radiate love all around me because it flows through me naturally. I radiate love through me because I love unconditionally. I radiate with love. I radiate with love. I RADIATE WITH LOVE!

Mirror Work. Repeat it.

For when we place our faith in Christ Jesus, there is no benefit in being circumcised or being uncircumcised. What is important is faith expressing itself in love.

Galatians 5:6 NLT

Help me to express what is important, and that is, faith expressing itself in and through love. Give me the faith, wisdom, and courage to radiate love to your people, Lord. Let your love come down and shine like no other because it is your loving touch that people need. I pray that people are open to receive your love. I pray that people are ready, able, and willing to receive you into their lives, Father and experience real love. In Jesus' Name, I Pray. Amen.

Taynia a. Mosley

"I RADIATE UNCONDITIONAL LOVE."

A 31 Day Love Transformation Prayer Devotional

Love Letter to Self

Taynia a. Mosley

A 31 Day Love Transformation Prayer Devotional

Love letter to God

Taynia a. Mosley

A 31 Day Love Transformation Prayer Devotional

DAY 14

"I AM NEEDED. I HAVE WORK TO DO!"

I am needed. I am loved. I add value to this world. Mirror Work – Repeat. Repeat. Repeat.

For I know the plans I have for you, declares the Lord, plans to prosper you and not to harm you, plans to give you hope and a future.

Jeremiah 29:11 NIV

Lord, only you know what is planned for my future. Help me to seek you first before making any major decisions in my life. I do not want to go left when I am supposed to go right. Lord, I need your guidance in my life. I need you to direct my path as your word says. I will be slow to speak and quick to listen in my life because my life is not my own. I need you! In Jesus' Name, I Pray. Amen.

Taynia a. Mosley

"I AM NEEDED. I HAVE WORK TO DO!"

A 31 Day Love Transformation Prayer Devotional

Love Letter to Self

Taynia a. Mosley

A 31 Day Love Transformation Prayer Devotional

Love letter to God

_____
_____
_____
_____
_____
_____
_____
_____
_____
_____
_____
_____
_____
_____
_____
_____
_____
_____
_____
_____
_____
_____
_____
_____
_____
_____
_____

Taynia a. Mosley

DAY 15
"I AM VALUABLE!"

Say it with me: I AM VALUABLE.

I bring plenty to the table because I am valuable. Everything I do adds value to my life and those around me.

Live a life filled with love, following the example of Christ. He loved us and offered himself as a sacrifice for us, a pleasing aroma to God.

Ephesians 5:2 NLT

Father, help me to see myself as you see me. Help me to see myself as valuable to this world. Help me to know that I am gifted and equipped to help your people here on earth. I know that I am needed, I am loved, and I am valuable to the people you have called me to. Lord, guide me to those people who I am called to in this season. In Jesus' Name, I Pray. Amen.

Taynia a. Mosley

"I AM VALUABLE!"

A 31 Day Love Transformation Prayer Devotional

Love Letter to Self

Taynia a. Mosley

A 31 Day Love Transformation Prayer Devotional

Love letter to God

Taynia a. Mosley

DAY 16

"I AM FILLED WITH THE VIBRATION OF LOVE!"

Get to the mirror, look deep into your eyes, and say the daily affirmation. Say it. Feel it. Own it.

My frequency is on the right vibration for love. I receive love because I am open to love.

Love never gives up, never loses faith, is always hopeful, and endures through every circumstance.

1 Corinthians 13:7

I am filled with the vibration of love because your love radiates my heart. I feel your love that surrounds me because it enwraps me when I need it the most. Lord, I pray that the love you give to me radiates so strong that it leaps through me onto all those that are around me, to those that are feeling lost, down, and out. I pray for those that are going through heartbreaks, I pray for those having a hard time to love or trust again. I pray for those that are hopeless. I pray for those that are hurting with devastation. I pray Lord that you will give them the peace that surpasses all understanding. Lord, comfort them in their time of need, give them strength, give them the courage to follow their hearts. In Jesus' Mighty Name, I Pray. Amen.

A 31 Day Love Transformation Prayer Devotional

"I AM FILLED WITH THE VIBRATION OF LOVE!"

Taynia a. Mosley

Love Letter to Self

_____
_____
_____
_____
_____
_____
_____
_____
_____
_____
_____
_____
_____
_____
_____
_____
_____
_____
_____
_____
_____
_____

A 31 Day Love Transformation Prayer Devotional

Love letter to God

A 31 Day Love Transformation Prayer Devotional

DAY 17
"I WELCOME LOVE WITH OPEN ARMS"

Here is a big one. Get to the mirror, look deep into your own eyes, and say the daily affirmation. Say it. Feel it. Own it. KNOW that you can receive love with open arms today and forever.

Never shut down on love because when you are open to love, it opens your spirit to always receive love. Always remember that love never shuts down on you.

God blesses those whose hearts are pure, for they will see God.

Matthew 5:8

My Lord, help me to see that I deserve love and that I should never give up on love. Love will never leave me because I know that in my heart of hearts, I choose to love freely and openly. I choose to love because those that need it will receive love from me. Lord, I want to be used by you because you are amazing. You seem to love us even when we don't love ourselves. Help me to receive love openly. Help me to know that I am worthy of all love. In Jesus' Mighty Name, I Pray. Amen.

A 31 Day Love Transformation Prayer Devotional

"I WELCOME LOVE WITH OPEN ARMS."

Love Letter to Self

___

A 31 Day Love Transformation Prayer Devotional

Taynia a. Mosley

Love letter to God

A 31 Day Love Transformation Prayer Devotional

DAY 18

"I DESERVE LOVE AND RECEIVE IT IN ABUNDANCE"

Do it now! Get to the mirror and say today's affirmation.

You deserve it, and you know it!

This is my commandment: Love each other in the same way that I have loved you. There is no greater love than to lay down one's life for one's friend.

John 15:12-13 NLT

Father, I know that I deserve love, but I do not always know how to receive love. Father, forgive me because you have made us experience love in the greatest way but the hurt and pain have somehow shut love out. I do not want to shut love out, I want to receive all that love has for me in my life. I want to give love, as you have commanded us to do. I pray for your guidance in this season of my life. Help me to stay open and not shut down when I feel low. I want to be an example of your love. Help me, Father, in this time of need, to keep being the light for your people. I know that every day will not be easy, so this is where I need your input to kick into my life. I need to hear from you in this season of my life. Help me to be strong so that I can be what your people need in this season. In Jesus' Name, I Pray. Amen.

Taynia a. Mosley

> "I DESERVE LOVE AND RECEIVE IT IN ABUNDANCE."

A 31 Day Love Transformation Prayer Devotional

Love Letter to Self

_____
_____
_____
_____
_____
_____
_____
_____
_____
_____
_____
_____
_____
_____
_____
_____
_____
_____
_____
_____
_____
_____
_____
_____
_____
_____
_____
_____

Taynia a. Mosley

A 31 Day Love Transformation Prayer Devotional

Love letter to God

_____

_____

_____

_____

_____

_____

_____

_____

_____

_____

_____

_____

_____

_____

_____

_____

_____

_____

_____

_____

_____

_____

_____

Taynia a. Mosley

A 31 Day Love Transformation Prayer Devotional

DAY 19
"LOVE IS ATTRACTED TO ME, AND I AM ATTRACTED TO LOVE"

Love is all around me because love chases me down. I exude love, I explore love, I choose love.

Do you really believe in love? Be honest with yourself today, and begin to believe in love, begin to accept the love that you deserve! Repeat. Repeat. Repeat.

Be careful not to practice your righteousness in front of others to be seen by them. If you do, you will have no reward from your Father in heaven.

Matthew 6:1 NIV

Father, help me to keep my mind and heart open to love. Please help me not to shut down and become bitter, I do not want to operate from a broken heart. Help me to keep my eye on the prize and that is to love your people. I know that you want us to love others, so that means others must love me. I need to receive love from others without expectations or fear of being rejected. I want to love everyone exactly how they are supposed to be loved and treat them how they are supposed to be treated. I am praying for people to love me in that same capacity. Fill my heart Lord with real love, help me to not hold back my feelings. Help me to grow in you and give people a chance to really love me. Heal my emotions. I pray away bitterness and broken heartedness and I loose the spirit of a sound mind, peace, and wholeheartedness. Thank you, Father, for the breakthrough to experience real love. I love you, Lord. I pray this prayer in Jesus' Mighty Name. Amen.

A 31 Day Love Transformation Prayer Devotional

"LOVE IS ATTRACTED TO ME, AND I AM ATTRACTED TO LOVE."

Taynia a. Mosley

Love Letter to Self

A 31 Day Love Transformation Prayer Devotional

Taynia a. Mosley

Love letter to God

A 31 Day Love Transformation Prayer Devotional

DAY 20

"LOVE FOLLOWS ME EVERYWHERE THAT I GO"

Love follows me everywhere that I go, it follows me every day of my life because I am love.

It is mirror time! REPEAT today's affirmation morning, noon, and night.

What a person desires is unfailing love; better to be poor than a liar.

Proverbs 19:22 NIV

I want to be kindhearted, oh God. I want people to truly know my heart. I want to desire love and to be loved. I want to desire kindness because it is imperative to your people. I do not want to be cold-hearted nor bitter. Search my heart, oh Lord, because there, in my heart, you will know my truth. I have been broken but I will not remain there. For your word says that you are close to the brokenhearted, and I know that to be true because you are a healer. Heal my heart and cleanse my soul to only walk in love and gratitude. Help me to see the good in every person that I run across. In Jesus' Name, I pray. Amen.

Taynia a. Mosley

"LOVE FOLLOWS ME EVERYWHERE THAT I GO."

A 31 Day Love Transformation Prayer Devotional

Love Letter to Self

Taynia a. Mosley

A 31 Day Love Transformation Prayer Devotional

Love letter to God

Taynia a. Mosley

DAY 21
"LOVE IS THE MOTIVE"

I've got love on my mind.

Look yourself in the eyes and say your affirmation over and over again.

Sensible people control their temper; they earn respect by overlooking wrongs.

Proverbs 19:11 NLT

Today I am thinking about love because I can feel God's love all over me. It enwraps me, it comforts me, it never lets me down. God, your love is unfailing, and you have proven that to me time and time again. Those nights when I didn't know how to love myself, it seems as if you kept me. Through all the breakdowns, the breakups, the drama, the loss of hope, the confusion, feeling as if I was not loved, the setbacks you have turned all that around for me. I thank you for the peace. I am so grateful that you did not give up on me because now I can help those around me that are broken, lost, hurt, and confused. I thank you for your strength, I thank you for shining your light on me. In Jesus' Name, I pray. Amen.

A 31 Day Love Transformation Prayer Devotional

"LOVE IS THE MOTIVE."

Taynia a. Mosley

Love Letter to Self

_____
_____
_____
_____
_____
_____
_____
_____
_____
_____
_____
_____
_____
_____
_____
_____
_____
_____
_____
_____
_____
_____
_____
_____
_____

A 31 Day Love Transformation Prayer Devotional

Taynia a. Mosley

Love letter to God

A 31 Day Love Transformation Prayer Devotional

DAY 22

"I DWELL IN LOVE."

I dwell in love, I stay there, I live there…

Mirror Work Time!

Do not conform to the pattern of this world, but be transformed by the renewing of your mind. Then you will be able to test and approve what God's will is - his good, pleasing, and perfect will.
Romans 12:2 NIV

Lord, I thank you for your perfect will and your perfect ways. I pray to always dwell inside of love; I pray to always stay in a place of love because God is love. I pray that my love comes off to people as pure because it comes from a pure place in my heart. I pray to always be open to receive love even in the most destructive days. I pray to never lose focus on what life is all about. I never want to lose focus on life. I know that every day will not be perfect, so I am praying that every day, I am willing to do the work to show myself approved. Help me to renew my mind daily so that I don't get caught up in the world's ways. In Jesus' Name, I Pray. Amen.

A 31 Day Love Transformation Prayer Devotional

"I DWELL IN LOVE."

Love Letter to Self

A 31 Day Love Transformation Prayer Devotional

Taynia a. Mosley

Love letter to God

A 31 Day Love Transformation Prayer Devotional

DAY 23

"I AM CREATED FOR LOVE"

I value love because love lives on the inside of me. I come from love; therefore, I was created with love.

Say it to yourself in the mirror without hesitation. Feel it, know it, believe the words that you are saying.

Let your favor shine on your servant. In your unfailing love, rescue me.

Psalms 31:16 NLT

Let your favor shine on me, your servant. In your unfailing love, Lord, rescue me. I need to see the value that lay on the inside of me. I need to know what I truly bring to the table, to this world. Lord, help me to find my purpose in life, help me to walk in your footsteps that you put out before me. I need to value love because that is who I truly am. Help me to see God on the inside of myself so that I can be confident; so that your people can truly see God down on the inside of me. I know what I was created for I just need your guidance on how to get myself there. Send people to lead me to my destiny when I can't see my way. I thank you now, Lord, because I know that you are working it out on my behalf for your people. In Jesus' Name, I Pray. Amen.

"I AM CREATED FOR LOVE."

A 31 Day Love Transformation Prayer Devotional

Love Letter to Self

Taynia a. Mosley

A 31 Day Love Transformation Prayer Devotional

Love letter to God

Taynia a. Mosley

A 31 Day Love Transformation Prayer Devotional

DAY 24

"I FEEL LOVED"

I feel loved because I am loved by many. I refuse to live my life feeling like I am alone.

Feel it, breathe it, release it into the atmosphere all day, today. Say it out loud. Let's work!

For where two or three are gathered together in my name, there am I in the midst of them.

Matthew 18:20 KJV

Lord, I just want to say thank you, Father, for releasing me from the feeling of loneliness because I know that I am not alone. I have love all around me. I thank you for teaching me how to embrace love, how to give love, and how to receive love. It has not always been easy, but I refuse to give up on love. I am open to loving and making better every relationship in my life. For your word says that when two or more are gathered, there you are in the midst. I am asking that you be in the midst of every relationship or situation that comes to hinder me. I pray a release of the spirit of love concerning all of my relationships, including family and friends, because we were put here on earth to love. I speak peace right now over all of my relationships. In Jesus' Mighty Name, I pray. Amen.

A 31 Day Love Transformation Prayer Devotional

"I FEEL LOVED."

Taynia a. Mosley

Love Letter to Self

A 31 Day Love Transformation Prayer Devotional

Love letter to God

A 31 Day Love Transformation Prayer Devotional

DAY 25

"I KNOW THAT I AM ENOUGH. I SHOW UP FOR MYSELF AND OTHERS"

When you know that you are enough, you become grateful.

Mirror Time. Let's Go!

Above all else, guard your heart, for everything you do flows from it. Keep your mouth free of perversity; keep corrupt talk far from it.

Proverbs 4:22-23 NIV

Dear Heavenly Father, I come to you today so humbled, and so grateful for life. I thank you for the peace that surrounds my soul. I am guarding my heart because that is in your word. I am guarding my heart against all evil - no evil shall come nigh me. I am protected by your love. I thank you, Father, for loving me and keeping me out of harm's way. I pray to continue to show up for myself and others while you direct my path. Show me what to say and what to do for others as they need it. Teach me your kind, loving ways to press upon your people. In Jesus' Mighty Name, I Pray. Amen.

Taynia a. Mosley

> "I KNOW THAT I AM ENOUGH. I SHOW UP FOR MYSELF AND OTHERS."

A 31 Day Love Transformation Prayer Devotional

Love Letter to Self

Taynia a. Mosley

A 31 Day Love Transformation Prayer Devotional

Love letter to God

Taynia a. Mosley

DAY 26

"I ONLY ATTRACT HEALTHY, LOVING RELATIONSHIPS"

It does not matter what type of relationship you encounter; you must know and believe that you only attract healthy, loving relationships into your life.

Mirror Time

But the Holy Spirit produces this kind of fruit in our lives: love, joy, peace, patience, kindness, goodness, faithfulness, gentleness, and self-control. There is no law against these things! Those who belong to Christ Jesus have nailed the passions and desires of their sinful nature to his cross and crucified them there. Since we are living by the Spirit, let us follow the Spirit's leading in every part of our lives.

Galatians 5:22-25 NLT

I pray for strength to exude me, Lord. I pray for patience in this season of my life. I pray that only healthy, loving relationships enter into my life because

I want to be surrounded by peace. I want to produce the fruits of your Spirit, I want people to know You by your fruit that flows from me. I always pray to have self-control inside of every relationship that I come into and the relationships that I have already built. I release all confusion and negativity out of my life, and I loose the power of clarity, understanding, and positive vibes into my life. I speak joy inside of my relationships, I speak trust inside of my relationships, I speak laughter inside of my relationships, I speak trust and understanding into my relationships. I thank you, Father, for your fruits that I carry down on the inside of me. I thank you that they are present and that people know that it all comes from you. Lord, I thank you for all of your mercy and your grace that is upon my life and those that surround me. I thank you for your forgiveness as I forgive those that have wronged me. I thank you, Holy Spirit, for always being present inside of my life. In Jesus' Mighty Name, I Pray. Amen.

A 31 Day Love Transformation Prayer Devotional

"I ONLY ATTRACT HEALTHY, LOVING RELATIONSHIPS."

Love Letter to Self

A 31 Day Love Transformation Prayer Devotional

Taynia a. Mosley

Love letter to God

DAY 27
"I AM SELFLESS"

I love myself and everybody else, and in return, everybody loves me.

Get in front of the mirror, and let's do the work.

Rejoice in the Lord always [delight, take pleasure in Him]; again, I will say, rejoice! Let your gentle spirit [your graciousness, unselfishness, mercy, tolerance, and patience] be known to all people. The Lord is near.

Philippians 4:4-5 AMP

Dear Lord, everybody in this world deserves to be loved, it is our birthright, but somehow there are people in this world struggling to be loved and treated right. I pray for those people who are searching for love but can't find it. I pray for those people who are lost in this world. I pray that they find your love in this season of their lives. I pray that you send them love and compassion because everyone needs it. Jesus, we need you. There are a lot of hurting people in this world, that are desperately searching for something;

they just don't know what it is they are looking for. We need your guidance and direction in this moment of our lives. We need your knowledge and wisdom in this area of our lives. We need your love. Lord, we need your protection everywhere that we go. I thank you, Father, for the turnaround. In Jesus' Mighty Name, I Pray. Amen.

Taynia a. Mosley

"I AM SELFLESS."

A 31 Day Love Transformation Prayer Devotional

Love Letter to Self

Taynia a. Mosley

A 31 Day Love Transformation Prayer Devotional

Love letter to God

Taynia a. Mosley

DAY 28
"I AM WORTHY OF LOVE"

I am worth it all. I deserve nothing but the best because I am God's best.

In front of the mirror is the only way that you can look yourself in the eyes, and here is where you can reach your inner self. Look into your eyes, touch your heart, and repeat today's affirmation until you truly believe it. You are worth it!

Then Jesus said, "Come to me, all of you who are weary and carry heavy burdens, and I will give you rest. Take my yoke upon you. Let me teach you because I am humble and gentle at heart, and you will find rest for your souls. For my yoke is to bear, and the burden I give you is light."

Matthew 11:28-30 NLT

Lord, you have deemed me worthy of it all, I praise your Holy name. Lord, you see in me what I can't seem to see in myself. Help me to see myself as you see me. Help me to know who I truly am in you. Grant me to see things your way; I don't want to look at myself in a negative view. I know there is more for me, but I need your guidance to get there. Lord, you are so worthy to be praised, and I can't thank you enough for loving me and for keeping me. Father, I love you; you are marvelous. In Jesus' Mighty Name, I Pray. Amen.

A 31 Day Love Transformation Prayer Devotional

"I AM WORTHY OF LOVE."

Taynia a. Mosley

Love Letter to Self

A 31 Day Love Transformation Prayer Devotional

Love letter to God

A 31 Day Love Transformation Prayer Devotional

DAY 29

"I AM HEALED"

Healing is my portion.

My heart is healed from all past hurt. I forgive everyone that has ever come against me.

Get rid of all bitterness, rage, anger, harsh words, and slander, as well as all types of evil behavior. Instead, be kind to each other, tenderhearted, forgiving one another, just as God through Christ has forgiven you.

Ephesians 4:31-32 NLT

I have been broken, Lord, and only you can heal me. Father, I ask that you touch my heart, that you mend my broken heart so that I can fully love again. Lift the heavy pressure of the world off my shoulders because I cannot stand on my own. I need your healing power to touch my heart, to help me to forgive. I want to forgive and no longer have the issue dwell in my heart, I want to completely turn it over to you. I no longer want to live in the past. I want to be free - free to heal, free to love, free to live, and free to just be me. I thank you, Father, for I know you have plans for my life, according to your word. I am ready to walk into my destiny. I am destined with a purpose, I am destined for greatness. I pray this prayer in Jesus' Name. Amen.

Taynia a. Mosley

"I AM HEALED."

A 31 Day Love Transformation Prayer Devotional

Love Letter to Self

Taynia a. Mosley

A 31 Day Love Transformation Prayer Devotional

Love letter to God

_____
_____
_____
_____
_____
_____
_____
_____
_____
_____
_____
_____
_____
_____
_____
_____
_____
_____
_____
_____
_____
_____
_____

Taynia a. Mosley

DAY 30
"I AM WHOLE. I AM COMPLETE."

Every situation and circumstance, I have walked through it with blind faith. Although I did not know at the time, Lord, you were right there with me.

You know the drill, so, get to the mirror and repeat today's affirmation. Play with the statement to make it your own. Do the work!

Dear brothers and sisters, when troubles of any kind come your way, consider it an opportunity for great joy. For you know that when your faith is tested, your endurance has a chance to grow. So let it grow, for when your endurance is fully developed, you will be perfect and complete, needing nothing.

James 1:2-4 NLT

Father, I just want to say thank you for your healing touch. Thank you for your miraculous transformation of the heart. I thank you for comforting me through the storm, even when I could not see you or feel you, you were there. I thank you for keeping me, protecting me, and touching my mind you are a mind regulator because you gave me peace. I could have lost it all but you kept me. I am so grateful for your unfailing touch. I am grateful for your unfailing love. Father, I thank you for total healing, restoration, and completeness in You. It is so, In Jesus' mighty name, I pray. Amen.

A 31 Day Love Transformation Prayer Devotional

"I AM WHOLE. I AM COMPLETE."

Love Letter to Self

A 31 Day Love Transformation Prayer Devotional

Taynia a. Mosley

Love letter to God

DAY 31

On today, the last day of this devotional, I want to take the time out to thank God for our spouses (if you are married). If you are not married, thank God for your spouse that is coming because the Bible states in Romans 4:17 to call those things which are not as though they were. It takes faith and will power, but you must stand on God's word. Last but not least, if you do not want to be married or you are not ready for a relationship, thank God for the total transformation of healing your heart. Remember to give thanks in all things that you do, for a grateful heart will open doors for more. I thank you for taking this journey with me. I love you all and most importantly, God loves you.

(Married or waiting to be married) My partner and I are a perfect match for each other. We are divinely connected. The love between us is divine.

(I am Healed) I am divinely healed, my heart is healed. I love myself unconditionally, and I love others unconditionally. I am doing the work to move forward. I believe in love because I am love.

Mirror Work is so important. Once you look yourself in the eyes, you get to look deep inside your soul and make a commitment to yourself. Let's work!

Day 31 Affirmations

"I AM DIVINE LOVE."

And God has given us his Spirit as proof that we live in him and he in us. Furthermore, we have seen with our own eyes and now testify that the Father sent his Son to be the Savior of the world. All who declare that Jesus is the Son of God have God living in them, and they live in God. We know how much God loves us, and we have put our trust in his love. God is love, and all who live in love live in God, and God lives in them. And as we live in God, our love grows more perfect. So we will not be afraid on the day of judgment, but we can face him with confidence because we live like Jesus here in this world. Such love has no fear, because perfect love expels all fear. If we are afraid, it is for fear of punishment, and this shows that we have not fully experienced his perfect love. We love each other because he loved us first. If someone says, "I love God," but hates a fellow believer, that person is a liar; for if we don't love people we can see, how can we love God, whom we cannot see? And he has given us this command: Those who love God must also love their fellow believers.

1 John 4: 13-21

Father, I pray for forgiveness for all of my sins, knowingly and unknowingly. Lord, I ask that you give me supernatural peace and love that wraps around me everywhere that I go. Lord, I thank You for divine love, divine healing, divine restoration, divine completeness, and divine peace to be able to love unconditionally. Lord, I thank you for your healing touch. I thank you for my marriage, I thank you for my loving spouse. I thank you for the turnaround. Lord, you have been too good to me and for that I am forever grateful and ready to be used by You. I thank You for this 31-day love transformation because this is what I truly needed to be free. In Jesus' Mighty Name, I pray. Amen.

A 31 Day Love Transformation Prayer Devotional

ABOUT THE AUTHOR

Author & Relationship Coach Taynia A. (Coleman) Mosley was born and raised out of Detroit, MI. She is the founder of Destined With A Purpose Blog and Coaching, she is also the author of 'An Unnecessary Breakdown Within Your Relationship.' These tools have helped heal people from broken relationships and broken hearts. Heartbreak is no game and can destroy a person if it is left unmended.

For more information visit:
www.destinedwithapurpose.com

or email
tayniacoleman@gmail.com.

www.ingramcontent.com/pod-product-compliance
Lightning Source LLC
Chambersburg PA
CBHW061300110426
42742CB00012BA/1993